GERARD MALANGA

MYTHOLOGIES OF THE HEART

By Gerard Malanga

3 Poems for Benedetta Barzini (1967)
Prelude To International Velvet Debutante (1967)
Screen Tests / A Diary, in collaboration with Andy Warhol (1967)
The Last Benedetta Poems (1969)
cristinas world (1970)
Gerard Malanga Selbsportrat eines Dichters (1970)
10 Poems For 10 Poets (1970)
the blue book (1970)
beatle calendar (1970)
chic death (1971)
poetry on film (1972)
Wheels of Light (1972)
The Poetry of Night, Dawn and Dream / Nine Poems for César Vallejo
     (1972)
A Portfolio of Four Duographs, in collaboration with A. T. Mann (1973)
Licht / Light (1973, bilingual)
7 Poems for Pilar Crespi (1973)
Incarnations: Poems 1965–1971 (1974)
Rosebud (1975)
Leaping Over Gravestones (1976)
Bringing Up Baby (1977)
Ten Years After: The Selected Benedetta Poems (1977)
100 years have passed (1978)
This Will Kill That (1983)
The Legacy of Gaile Vazbys (1983)
Three Diamonds (1991)
Cinéma parlant (feature-length screenplay, 1993)
Mythologies of the Heart (1996)

Selected Compilations

Transatlantic Review #52—An Anthology of New American Poetry (1975)
Little Caesar #9 / "Unprecedented Information" (1979)
Angus MacLise Checklist 1959–1979 (1981)
UP-TIGHT: The Velvet Underground Story (with Victor Bockris, 1983)
Scopophilia: The Love of Looking (1985)

GERARD MALANGA

MYTHOLOGIES
OF THE HEART

BLACK SPARROW PRESS   SANTA ROSA   1996

ACKNOWLEDGMENTS

Grateful acknowledgment is made to the following publications in which some of these poems first appeared (some in somewhat different form): *Arshile* #3, *Artes International* (The Swedish Academy), *Bakunin*, *Caliban* #15, *Cholla*, *Cover* (Vol. 5/#2), *Deadstart*, *Electric Rexroth* (Kobe, Japan), *Exquisite Corpse* (Vol. 8/#5–9), *First Intensity* #2, *Friction*, *Harvard Review*, *Ignite* #1, *Jane* #3, *Machete*, *Michigan Quarterly Review*, *Nexus*, *The North Stone Review* #13, *Project Papers* (Vol. 1/#31), *Santa Monica Review*, *Tarasque* #1, *The Cafe Review* (Vol. 3/#6) and *20 Jaar Paard* (Den Haag, Nederland).

An excerpt from "Things to Remember About TRI-X" appears on Broadshirt/Akashic issue #2.

Acknowledgment is also made to Black Sparrow Press for its use of "First Poem for Isabel Garcia-Lorca de los Rios" in its serial pamphlet publication *Sparrow* (#35), Copyright © 1975 by Gerard Malanga, and for "Andrea Bankoff, from a Letter postmark December 4, 1963—Beverly Hills," in *Three Diamonds* (Black Sparrow Press) Copyright © 1991 by Gerard Malanga; to Any Art (Den Haag, Nederland) for its publication of "In the Kaaterskill" in a limited edition broadside Copyright © 1992 by Gerard Malanga; to Temple Press Ltd. (Brighton, U.K.) for its use of "Snow Emergency Street," "Lorna Hopper, Miss April Playmate of the Month," "A Day Like Any Other:" and "Poem in the Manner of Ted Berrigan" in its publication, RATIO: 3/MEDIA SHAMANS (1991) Copyright © 1991 by Gerard Malanga.

All photo-inserts © by Gerard Malanga.

Cover art image by Gerard Malanga based on a photograph by Nadar, "Mimi"—ca. 1856–59.

Reproduction of "The Meeting of Dante and Beatrice," by Henry Holiday, courtesy of The Board of Trustees of the National Museums & Galleries on Merseyside (Walker Art Gallery, Liverpool, U.K.).

Black Sparrow Press books are printed on acid-free paper.

LIBRARY OF CONGRESS CATALOGING-IN-PUBLICATION DATA

Malanga, Gerard.
   Mythologies of the Heart / Gerard Malanga.
     p.   cm.
     ISBN 0-87685-994-5 (cloth trade : alk. paper). — ISBN 0-87685-995-3 (signed cloth : alk. paper). — ISBN 0-87685-993-7 (pbk. : alk. paper).
     I. Title.
PS3563.A42M98   1996
811'.54—dc20   95-53182
                                                 CIP

for

Ted ...   Ted Berrigan

When you are in love
all of the time
            you get bored   *because*
                                      life
            when it's always the same
                                                is boring
      isn't it?
            that's a strange theory

                        from "Tambourine Life"

TABLE OF CONTENTS

III—THE ODEON TEXT

IV—SIGHTINGS

V—FASHION SECRETS

MYTHOLOGIES *of the* HEART

The Meeting of Dante and Beatrice, by Henry Holiday

Dante and Beatrice first met when they were nine years old. The second meeting, depicted by the artist, took place years afterwards in a street in Florence; but although they did not speak, and, indeed, it is doubtful whether they ever spoke, Beatrice's image was engraven on Dante's heart until his death.

I

TWO OR THREE GIRLS I ONCE KNEW

All my life I have been haunted by the obsession that to desire a thing or love a thing intensely is to place yourself in a vulnerable position, to be a possible, if not probable, loser of what you most want.

—Tennessee Williams

Andrea Bankoff
    from a Letter postmark   December 4, 1963—
    Beverly Hills.

I was suppose to write
but didn't.

As always one is distracted.

Yet some sense

specific

to who you are

remains :

night spent in your parents' attic

the warm flesh
beside me

the bare mattress

the bits and pieces
of conversation,

the contact-sheet of you
naked, the firm breasts.

Wordsworth's "recollection

in tranquility,"

the key to finding you—

nothing to go on now

4:viii:81 nyc

FIRST POEM FOR ISABEL GARCÍA-LORCA DE LOS RIOS

---

the blood of a poet flows thru your veins
your hair expresses the wind
by love for the flesh

sweet rain hits my eyes and head
buildings sunset against the red
in rosecolored sky

inside pocket of charms
let whatever discloses itself be seen
against the grain of a large city dream

10:vi:69 nyc

how
far away
are you

how far
away are
you

for Spot

for Kate

nineteen sixty-eight

Gotham
Book
Mart

N Y C

hair in braids

Arm
in cast—

or was it
leg

can't remember now

•

your dad
snowed in
at Buffalo

It's fifteen
minutes
past eight

getting late

can't wait
any longer

this fact of things

having to
get somewhere

what is found there

how it begins
or ends there

how much time
is there
left

5:xii:77 nyc

Tabula Rasa

We are strangers to each other
yet, that of all women
it shld have been her,
not telling her—not knowing
where to reach her—it was a poem
I was interested in and one
not written yet. This is
the Past of what is now
the Present. Brooklyn, early as 1959.
END. Scene shifts to Cincinnati
and then back to Greenwich Village—
this time living with "lover"
—presumably married—
and then there be 20 years,
that the soul be naked
at the end of time.
Stop right there, said Time.

A FOOTNOTE TO THE ABOVE,
              I can see her now.

Please excuse this intrusion.

The density of events that followed

at the

turning of hallway staircase leading to alley

and pausing

and going under.

for Carol Chalik

16:i:80

Asleep at last:

Jung's four functions—

thinking

feeling

sensation

intuition

"The Art of Observable Dreams"

Days, weeks, months,
sometimes years.

•

Having come thus far

"Underground Woman"

by

Kay Boyle

Faith ... Faith Franckenstein,

her daughter;

only child
by that marriage.

Where had she been
inside my psyche?

Letters

photographs

that useful
sense of past.

Wordsworth's "recollection
in tranquility" come true:

Borough of Richmond—1962

black pebble beach, South Beach

the Narrows

fucked

afraid to come,
at first,

but did, finally.

Swam in total darkness. Opaque night

No swimsuit

no moonlight

no one else

no afterthoughts,
but now

circumstance of time

sitting cold wind back

Dried off
on towels

stolen
from
dorm

nearby college

top of
Grymes
Hill

Later,
back somehow
to winding road,

Bay Street.

Chill in air now

edge of
woods
asleep.

4:vi:78 South Beach, S.I.

Whereabouts Unknown

Anne van der Hoof. Met at the 2nd annual NY Bookfair.
Niece of a former governor of Colorado. We raptured each other
standing up on the Esplanade under parklight in Bklyn Hts.
Said she'd write. She never did. (Who would?!) Moved.
Left no forwarding address.

Lize Thulin, student at Simon's Rock. Parents living in
Paris. Brief encounter, Melvin's Drugstore, Gt. Barrington,
June, 1973.

Deirdre LaPorte, one-time member of rock group known as
Stoneground; went off to New Mexico. A couple of notes.
Then nothing.

Carolyn DeBenden, fashion model. Never spoke to each other,
though she was girlfriend of a friend. Burnt out in New York.
Returned to Paris.

Janet, niece of poet Bill Hunt's wife, Marjorie. Chicago,
June, 1973. Long shiny black hair and brackets on teeth.
Left note on bed which read:

> "I would like to touch your hand,
> your face and talk of gentle things—
> now I am alone."

Susan Quick, b. March 20, 1943, my birth-date, chance meeting
Alice's Thanksgiving feast, Stockbridge School, 1971.

Bobbi Shaw, Max's Kansas City, Fall, 1966.
Wrote me my first fan letter. On her way to Hollywood.

Andrea Bankoff, Sept. 1963. Party on the Santa Monica Pier.
Went back to motel room. Andy trying to break thru chain
on door while in bed. He's pissed. Dress quickly. Went to
her parents' home in L A . Up all night in attic. Morning.
Catch bus back to Santa Monica. Half-asleep on beach
while Andy reads reviews of Elvis paintings outloud to himself.
Three years later we return to L A . A different scene entirely.
Went to visit. No name on door. Found no one home.

Carol Chalik, teenage romance, circa 1960 Bklyn, staring out
in photo-machine forever.

31:i:76 nyc

f-stop

October 1, 1983

n y c

the ⎫ to
morning ⎬ remember it
after ⎭ all

or

in retrospect :

"tossing
and
turning"

you sd

the month,
August

inside out ,

or

likewise

the dark night of the soul

"vice
versa

and

vice versa"

you sd.

for Gaile Vazbys

Dark side of Self

for Victoria

I don't know
what to
         write
about you

         the photo
of a young girl
standing btn
windswept
clotheslines

doesn't exist
                   and
someone, resembling you
turned on stomach,
asleep and the
light from the window
outlines the curve
and small of the
back
         so I'll include
         that.

There is a cool
breeze I recall

and the
windswept
hair and

the sound
of wch
has nothing
to do
        with
any kind of
conclusion

or

        those
        rules

I break by
the way the
lines break.

26:iii:86 nyc

A DAY LIKE ANY OTHER :

I hadn't seen her for some time.
A few scant sightings
along Broadway/Lafayette
barely a hello as she passed, as if
I'd done something terribly wrong
and was not to be forgiven
when, in fact,
I'd done nothing
                except
to acknowledge
                her existence,
then as now—
                acknowledge the
personal history between us,
not take back what's lost,
but to celebrate that
part of the self shared with her existence,
to say *I know you and will forever know you.*
Likewise the reader.

Sunday, April Fool's Day,
to be exact,
waiting in line
at Instant Copy,
I noticed across from me

a rather tall and unusual-looking girl
long in the face
and that she was dressed entirely in black,
black stockings, black shit-kicker boots
short black mini, revealing taut thighs—
checkin out the small of her back,
the profile-cut as it were, attitudinal stance,
and not instantly recognizing it *was* her
until some time had passed—seconds ... was it minutes ?—
and that the hair was no longer Baltic blonde,
but dyed black w/ henna afterglow.

    As she spoke, I could barely make out
the voice : Gaile Vazbys—wldnt ya know
it—the way I remember her
speaking to me
over breakfast
teenage weekends   New York.

No apparent physical change,
'cept to experience her as her Other, as instant copy,
as someone else entirely,
separate from who she was to me, then as now.

    And kept thinking how the
denial of
personal history,
the poems defined
by her existence, defined
in her absence,
         exist apart
          from her,

        mythify her existence.
The myth clearly undenied.
Myth as Reality.
        Myth in my heart.

No words exchanged.
We never crossed eyes,

as if we never existed
in each other's presence
for those few brief moments
but in the realm of the unattainable,
now attained.

There's a poem somewhere in all this.

1:iv:90 nyc

> ... there shall be of my own creating a face
> beyond all others beautiful because of the soul
> which lives purely behind it.
>
> —*William Carlos Williams,*
> *from a letter.*

TO A YOUNG GIRL

For 100 years the word *soul* was mistranslated
as "mind" in Freud's papers
                    in the
                    original
German. When does the body become conscious?

The door opens. A young girl enters and looks slowly

around. Pictures brilliant on the wall. One man sitting in a chair.

Two figures silently standing. It is late afternoon. The girl is tall

with golden black hair and her eyes have a bluish glow.

They suggest the sky in all its timelessness.

                                        End of Dream
                                        into the Future.

Q: What is myth?

A: The eye

    as focus

    takes in

    remembering
           you   It is not with conceit
                 that I acknowledge you

                 but with
                 an optical
                 point–of–view
                 as such

               •

                 To say your face is timeless
                 is not conceit
                 but to register
                 that wch is elusive
                 as clouds in the
                 Saratoga twilight

                 and to attempt a new
                 kind of
                 sentiment
                         such as had
                              not been

                                expressed
since Dr. Williams
witnessed Isadora Duncan
dance in 1908.

But you, for the most
part, wld not
need to
know that   wld not need
                                    to know
                                    that contact
                                    with the eyes
                                    is all we have

•

I've spent the entire afternoon

attempting to put you in this poem

Out at Sodus Point

a rainstorm,

from seemingly nowhere

and with its accompanying light,

comes off the flat of

                Lake Ontario

You are
somewhere
in all this

22:v:87
Fairport, NY

POEM IN THE MANNER OF TED BERRIGAN

Anne Kepler
"... killed by smoke-poisoning while playing
the flute at the Yonkers Children's Hospital
during a fire set by a 16 year old arsonist ... 1965":

Ted Berrigan.
I might be one of the few
remaining friends who
actually did meet his "girl"
in the early morning rain
the sun coming up
warm from coffee
and now he's dead too
and the rest is
history.

4:v:90
Great Barrington, MA

BARZINI'S DAUGHTER

"You should have seen me papa
In my gym class falling to the floor.
I was so graceless; but I am fast learning.
I have to touch things and then draw the line.
I want to go to New York to model enough to study
Acting seriously and everything else, too.
I want to go over the hill today and look around me
At the landscape and the sea.
I want you to come with me papa
if you're not busy."

It's autumn, it's winter.
You look for yourself, the way you looked
As a child, in the "4 for a quarter" photos
Taken today. The light flashing behind your head
Pressed against my left shoulder
And a still-portrait emerges.
The landscape inserted behind us.
The clouds fairly bright in the late afternoon.

3:v:92 nyc

It's the first anniversary of November 8, 1966.
It's time to get the mail, walk the Lungotevere delle Armi.
It's time to read books, meet Elsa Morante
for lunch.

At the tabacchi a face appears
in the bi-monthly pages of *Vogue*.

On black-and-white film the same face wavers
and never disappears.

The young boy always remembers you
that way.

In the Republic of Italy he makes an awkward bow.

8:xi:67 Rome

> A director is a man, therefore he has ideas; he is also an artist, therefore he has imagination. Whether they are good or bad, it seems to me that I have an abundance of stories to tell. And the things I see, the things that happen to me, continually renew the supply.
>
> —*Michelangelo Antonioni*

Snow Emergency Street

All I know is this slow exhibition of greatness.
A description of what's been
Happening. The pain is not
Clearly defined. These are
The eyes of the young girl and that side of her
Character capable of being
Afraid. Across street young man walks
Back with hands in pockets.
Children's voices at playground
In distance. The sound
Track of tire treads making sharp turns
In the distance.
Water sprinkler being turned off.
A roadway ribbed with white lines where no one is
Crossing. In its beginning was its end.
A woman, a city, an intellect.
The environment of that experience.

Afer the affirmations
Who will discover the rejections?

for Benedetta

28:x:67 nyc

SONNET: GIVE IT A NAME

The optimism of remembering oneself;
Tomorrow different from today
And the night before.
Her other self under strobes,
And what's living undergoes
"Change" in sunlight, in candlelight.

She remembered herself bleeding
For the first time
In five years and, for the first time,
Believed in her feelings.
Tomorrow different from tonight and the day
Before: Gerard and Benedetta
Undergoing change in each other's arms.

Her head fit in the curve of my neck in the morning.

9:iii:67 Ann Arbor, MI

A MEETING IN NORTHAMPTON

Endless
expectations

endless
ways

I might
encounter you

are various.

Place of
"meaningful coincidence,"
as it were: a path
leading to a branch
of the Westfield River.

Sense of time and/or

place in passing

fixed in the mind.

•

We are back
where we started:
Northampton.

Wind shifts
the trees. Leaves
scurry along cement walk.

No chance
meeting anywhere
seems likely now.

•

Keep walking
kicking leaves
in the air.

Brown eyes.
Black hair.

That's how I remember you,
kicking leaves in the air.

I remember you,
I want to.

A woman now.

for Pip Ross

15:xi:75 nyc

Alighieri woke me this morning, saying
"All loves are blessed, Gerard.
The other day I was reading
La vita nuova and I thought of you,
you and the two
or three girls you once knew
head & shoulders
heart on fire
water and air."

Dante closes his cape in the photograph—

tells me, "Gerard, go back to sleep
now. See you again—somewhere, somehow."

I reach back as far as that day
when Beatrice
passed Dante on the Ponte Vecchio

Beatrice remembered by the words of Dante

would be about 700 years old today.

I've got a day to get through
and tomorrow
another. A wind moves
not into autumn into this poem.

Thursday already and I haven't had a cigarette in days.

5:ii:70 nyc

Someone has written
on the wall of the
flat I've just moved into,
nothing lasts.

2:x:73
Cambridge, MA

II

MAY 2, 1992

As Clement Greenberg said of James Agee, ca. 1939: "the ability to be sincere without being honest" is very much the point.

There's a scene where Dr. Yurii Zhivago
is seated at writing desk
and branches are rattling the windowpanes
and gusts of snow
blowing every which way
in the yard.

There's a close-up
words inked
on the white paper

Lara is asleep in one of the upstairs rooms.
The Urals blanketed in white.

You would think all this
were more than enough for a poem.

But wait. It's Spring now
in the Kaaterskill
and all this is happening
somewhere else.

3:v:92 Fultonham, NY

> You will hear, coming from within, a voice
> that leads to your destiny. It is the voice of desire,
> and not that of any desirable being.
> —*Georges Bataille*

THE LITTLE SCHOHARIE

The route of
the M. & S. Railroad
coming from within ...

for miles in a north-south direction
nothing
but broken-up ties, a faint echo.

So ... coming down from Vromans, Davis Crossing,

I've got to believe you don't exist.

You don't mind, do ya ?

The hum of an insect,
the tremor of uncut grass.
Kitchen table. The mountain covered in mist.
The purples and grey-greens of flowers.

CUT: Night falls. The moon disappears.
You represent more the im(age) of beauty

in erotic terms: You appear
open-minded, dreamlike, deserving
of a poem. How presumptuous of me.
Not everyone wants to be written about,
no matter how sincere
the intention. What makes this any different
from let's say how Courbet's *Le Sommeil* (1866)
is viewed, or the violence of an embrace, known as *rapture*
seduction and passion.

I take nothing for granted.
I take my mind off the mundane.
I try visualizing what your paintings might be
the moment before stepping into the studio,
all light and air, the smell of turp,
an oak floor, a low armchair,
cat purring
unsized canvas rolled up in corner,
military jetstream on distant horizon,
a slight rain, then no rain,
an open field sloping out back into a lap,
the dusty yard, chickens, or was that
the eternal part of the dream where suddenly
you're no longer "separate,"
as in "separate realities,"
but submerged
into
the four o'clock light.
Speck of paint on brow. Perspiration
wiped clean. Blue Navy workshirt
unbuttoned, catching the light.
What am I getting at, you wonder.

Simply that the eyes are
what the soul sees through,
or some such thing,
if I remember correctly
Ezra Pound's remark
is another way stating
Are you as smart as you look, or are looks deceiving,
like the bones in a face. Hence my gaze
is fixed. Hence the wind from the south side
is writing these lines.
The Schoharie below is a mirror
on the wall opposite. Your eyes close
the book in your lap.
The sky empties.

    I'd rather deny this poem
's existence, so that the desire would cease,
so that the erotic moment would cease.

17:ii:92
Great Barrington, MA

MEMORIAL DAY

Two used condoms,
almost saffron in color,
get trashed finally—

forgotten I'd put them
in desk drawer—a window

now looking out at East Mountain,
a hill really,
when suddenly I look inward:

the weekend before
hands clasping breasts
from behind full moon
out same window

My young Siamese, Archie
licks his black balls, anus, rolls
over in framed sunlight
reflected on floor,

goes cross-eyed,

meditates.

24:v:92
Great Barrington, MA

Tutto questo tempo

Puccini, "La Bohème"

and Mick …   Mick Jagger/Dave Stewart *say you will*

apropos

       "emotion recollected in tranquility"—

near or far I don't know.

The clock's ticking

the clock won't stop

We go on living

           the dream

or the dream

subsumes us,

outlives us, reawakens

         a hillock of sunlight

out back — Pictures for a Sunday Afternoon — in what's said

or not said ...

to be believed ?

Now I wonder.

There's a wise man sd

"We live as we can. Each day another— there is

no use in counting." There is

a picture had in the mind,

to be taken,

yet to be taken.

7:v:92
Great Barrington, MA

> Do I know who "she" is who "never
> responded"?
>
> *J.J. to G.M., from a letter*

HOW THEY DIDN'T MEET

She never responded to his pkge the 11th Apr '92—

the Gagosian catalogue, Jasper Johns's "According
to What," which dates from 1964—
                                        and so
she never sent
the postcard, thanking him
with her
phone number on the 15th,

so there was no way he cdve called then
to set up the rendezvous—the meeting itself—
the night of May 2nd Woodstock

and it hadn't rained as predicted
that night after all, a backroad
to Schoharie County
likewise instant rapport
because
next day he headed
north to Barrington
by way of connecting bus

thru Albany
and then on to Pittsfield ... the window
reflecting
        the inside out
on his face in the movable light ...
and the light begins to fade,

so none of what they'd
experienced or the morning after
had ever occurred

—not the Beaujolais '88
not the thraldom
not the bath the soapy insides,
Turkish towels the head
birdlike catching the light
not the kissing of feet ...

not the scent flesh on flesh makes ...

and there is no wind shhhhhhh in the spruce out back

no sun hiding in tree behind cloud

and that ... and that his letter 4 May
and her hand-painted card, also 4 May
never crossed in the post ...

that much is certain,

or her letter May 7th,
inadvertently dated April,

and the phone-call wch followed are hearsay

and the night of the full moon
the 16th is hearsay ...

all is hearsay

virtually no reference
among his papers
that would lead one
to surmise
it had been otherwise

nothing to link them

... and Beatrice Portinari
is not all in pure white,
between two older ladies,

—is not crossing the Ponte Vecchio, ca. 1283,
wch wdve made her eighteen,

but as figment of Alighieri's imaginings,

or had she passed thru—the wildflower
scent in her hair—
it wdve been at a time
he was elsewhere in Florence

and so
would not have known
how she appeared or what was not said

in the language of eyes meeting eyes

take back what is lost
give back what is gained

or Nora ... Nora Barnacle was her name—
or it might have been some other girl
waiting to cross not redhead
but raven haired we don't know
a few seconds making all seem (im)possible
for that matter a street in Dublin
on a day unlike another, June 16th,
to be exact, 1904

and the street is lost and the people in it

and Jap asks, "According to what?"

29:vi:92
Great Barrington, MA

> Success in the end
> eclipses the mistakes along the way.
>
> —*Chinese Fortune Cookie*

"ALL OF THIS OR NOTHING"

---

focus
for remembering
it all,

i.e.,

a mental picture.

Now it's autumn

fading Berkshire hills.

Grey mist
rising from
Green River,

quieter now
that winter
is approaching.

The light fading

faint echoes
no words,
then nothing.

Reflections.

The wind
lost now.

•

Try to imagine
voices in the distant present

across Catskills
and beyond

Try to
imagine
grey-shifting
clouds,

the head
back-lit.

Try to
imagine
you

as you

used
to be

hair shorn
to one side

or else
suddenly

the face
aglow,

eyes smiling,

comforting,

looking
into
the
camera.

Try to
imagine
what had
never been ...

might be

Try to
imagine

had you
not existed,

so these poems
before all else
had not existed.

•

It's the
quality
of time
counts

not its range
as in
days, years
months, weeks

scrambled

but of a morning
like none previous

mist burning away
against a
space of trees,

no clouds

sun somewhere east

•

Grey-brown
covers empty hills.

No grass, no leaves.

Things get left out

place in time.

What point
in stopping
here to ask:

So where are you now,

or were we never there ?

1992
Great Barrington, MA

Beatrice passing beyond the moment of meeting
so that all eyes looked elsewhere, so that
all thought of a text, such as *La vita nuova*,
or Joyce's *Ulysses*, need not have ever existed,
except by word
of mouth only, except as myth
would have it—
all of what's perceived
is to be believed,
leading you to draw
otherwise hasty conclusions.

What's left to the eyes, the nose?
What to Jim on a Dublin street? What to anyone?

1992
Great Barrington, MA

III

THE ODEON TEXT

Because desire is defined as the pursuit of that which is always already lost, the failure of desire is not its end, but its perpetuation.

—Terence Diggory,
"The Virgin"
from *William Carlos Williams and the Ethics of Painting*

Photo © by Gerard Malanga, 1981

SIGHTING, 1:30 a m, May 3rd 1981—the Odeon—name
unknown, with semiotexts spliced into infrastructure.

(tech-format: 3-second interval between bracketed *Pause* indicators.)

My subject is this: There is the look that lasts but an instant,
                              wch is in "an instant of time"[1]—
so-called sidewise glance—does not conceal itself
and yet wants to see and not be seen.
                              Such gestures,
a motion of the hand, a turn of the head,
                              hint a profound significance
The moment that in passing away remains,
                              and in remaining
passes away. "Beautiful things don't last
forever" was all Elsa[2] could tell me,
                              Via del Oca, 1968.

                              I take walks
for long hours
                 through the city streets;

it is the longing to penetrate the invisible
                 in order to see the visible—

---

1. Ezra Pound (See p. 80 of this text for complete statement).
2. Elsa Morante, poet novelist. Author of *La Storia: Romanzo,* Torino,
Einaudi Editore, 1974.

the *innigkeit*, as it were.

It is the longing to return to
                    the solitude of a mountain
                when the seasons change.

          I have a confession to make:
my most unselfish act has been to know how to conceal
from myself that it was I
who created what I admired.   [Pause]

                    Likewise the sense for the real
            is the means of acquiring
                    the power to shape things
                according to my wish.   [Pause]

A situational integrity.
Or Pound saying—what's he saying?—: "the
CONtinuous effort to have it different somewhere or other."[3]

                This is more of a
            psychological inspiration
                    than anything else. An intellectual pain.

        luce intellettüal piena d'amore.[4]

---

3. Ezra Pound, "Canto XCVII."
4. *Paradiso*, Canto XXX, Dante Alighieri, "We are come to the heaven which is a pure light—intellectual light full of love."
    Variant: "The intellectual love of a thing consists in understanding its perfections."—Spinoza.

This belief in the person
in a way she herself never dreamed of existing so intensely—

but more, belief in the event itself.

Approx. 1:30 a m,

variable cloudiness with gradual clearing—windy
with low readings in the mid-sixties.
The outlook for tomorrow ... mostly sunny skies, but all that
can change.

[Pause]

Is it not illusion, then, to take for cause
that wch rises to consciousness as an act of will?

One must not remove the aim from the total condition.
And yet the aim is, in this instance, not just an act of will
but desire also. And whosoever "desires" is affected,
i.e., "I desire you; you are worth knowing," whereas

I don't search for things in order
to explain why something occurs

but rather, change occurs, however slightly,

because all conscious purposes, all evaluations
are not perhaps the only means thru wch something
essentially different from what appears in consciousness
is achieved.

What is achieved by fulfilling desire

is by not fulfilling it
in by who's seen initially
retaining
somewhat of a mystique—evanescent, incomprehensible—
and "the innocence of becoming"
within a continuous present

So the impossible is not impossible:

the self freely willing its future
existence with someone
at the moment at wch
the possibility of that person
presently exists—

the freedom to choose—

responsibility
and adventure

a risk
and a challenge.

There are no
solutions,

there are only exceptions—

something that wants to occur interprets
the value of whatever else wants to occur
becomes more profound

In the *Bardo Thödol*[5] it is said that if the mind be fixed
  on the acquirement of any object, that object will be attained.

And so I seek a conception of the world
that takes this knowledge into account:

> a chance
> of eyes even.
> A passing glance.
>
> An interest,
>
> a tension,
>
> a hope—no, not a hope,
>
> almost a
>   certainty.

These are the minimal necessities
  of a passionate life
        and within
context of what's proposed
        as possibility—the adventure of choice
                (= *krino*)

---

5. Apocryphal literature of Tibetan Buddhism (in Tibetan, *Thos-grol*.
Section X).

There has been a rain
but the cobblestones
are still wet. Silent. Immovable. The Rainbow comes and goes.

Appennini
in pale blue mist

pocked, muddied floes
on the Arno

glow
for several seconds
each morning

until they no longer exist.

Via Tornabuoni

Porta Romana

Viale dei Collo.

The year, ca. 1283, Firenze.
The second of possibly three sightings
both outside and inside the mind;
this one on Ponte Vecchio—
the attitude of looking and waiting:

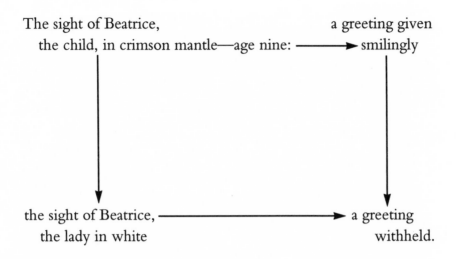

The sight of Beatrice,   a greeting given
   the child, in crimson mantle—age nine: ⟶ smilingly

  the sight of Beatrice, ⟶ a greeting
     the lady in white   withheld.

... dove 'l sol tace[6]

Then everyone goes away.

[Fade-out

I had nothing to do with it.
I was not there. I was not born.

The invention of photography hadn't occurred.

There were no eye-witness accounts.

I did not arouse those so-called "beautiful feelings"
I do not arouse them now.

---

6. "*là dove il sol tace* ... to where the sun is silent," *Inferno*, Canto I, Dante Alighieri (Variant: Homer, *The Odyssey*).

This desire still isn't immortal enough,

is inexpressible
because
the words
no longer
call forth the
vision wch the
person herself
wld call forth

This is my last sighting—this place, this voice.
I stop listening, look away.

Such is choice
self-recognition begins to feel
as a trace of intuited
eternity sensed in time

isolated moment as image

the movement of
the ego in time,

i.e., "the eternal *now*"[8]

"… that which presents an intellectual and emotional complex in an instant of time."[7]

---

7. Ezra Pound, "A Retrospect" (1916), from *The Literary Essays of Ezra Pound*, NY, New Directions, 1934.
8. Robbe-Grillet, Alain, *Pour un nouveau roman*, p. 134, Paris, Gallimard, 1963.

the survival of one's past and
the survival of one's self
in the memory of others.

The necessity of continuing.

Such was the history and
                    the limit of her life

Such is the data of psychic experience.
Such are the repeated tellings—

To love implies the knowledge that love ends
because the lover becomes a squanderer, intoxicated.
Everything else is the language of the silent
young woman who sits at a table across from me
at the Odeon in Tribeca almost seven hundred
years after
              because
when I look at her I feel
my immortality upon me
                         and as a great weight,
                         because what often overwhelms
                         is the memory that
                         what's strived for now
                         may have been nearer, truer,
                         and it's attachment
                         infinitely tender, at some other time.

And this is a field in wch
flowers endlessly open

and this is the continuous
transformation
in wch
the seed falls and evolves,

          turns into summer, grows in the mouth.

So this is the old occult saying unrehearsed: for every human
being is a series of events wch cannot coincide with any other
because each occurs within different temporal progress and
      continua.

Or, likewise, Rilke's Sonnet 20/2nd series—"… nowhere does the
                    circle close."

Elsewhere it's sd: "A line can only be aware of another line
            at the point of contact … and a soul
          of another soul."[9]

The poem becomes witness and lyrical interference,

      so-called "postponed destiny" Lawrence proposes,

      "a dialectical lyric"[10]

      the measure and rhythm of walking

          the impulse to go,

----

9. Aleister Crowley.
10. Kierkegaard.

to turn,

to stand still   in streets,

in parks,

along
Lungotevere delle Arno

that is, seeks,

continuously intervenes

to include
the intimidation her spirit evokes.

Beauty stands knee-deep in a freshwater pond.

"Beauty stands in admiration of weak minds
led captive" John Milton wrote.

Beauty both
intimidates
and flatters
the senses.

"Beauty, powerless
and helpless,

hates understanding"[11]

Beauty can kill.

But we forget easily.

I decide that
beauty is
friendly.

All at once I understand
the slow, solemn motion of the clouds at 4 p m, and
I understand waves going out from the shore
and always another sound—the heavy roar
of the surf farther out

                    and the silence
            close to shore is the silence in me
        after I return from a walk up the beach.

I sit at my desk. I'm awake now. It's raining lightly.

Two hours have gone by. All seems calm

and yet somewhere inside I am not calm.

---

11. J. B. Baillie.

By nightfall the whispering
voices I heard earlier
                    in the dusk on the road
have transformed themselves
                    into the rustling of leaves.

I want to believe that you're still months away—

that you endure
          just as you are,
          in the invisible

and unlike a star that vanishes and can't be brought back—

that way I don't need
to think about you

that way I become always equal to
accident—
               that is, to be unprepared
          so to be master of my fate / master of my depths also

I want to believe
that to be opposites
always, and nothing but opposite,
is not unfavorable.

I want to believe
that you don't appear to me
as I wish you to be

I want to believe that beauty
is the highest quality
to wch art may aspire,

                but that is erroneous

I want to believe that when I inquire
about you, it is that what art may be,
life of course can be also

[Pause]

I want to believe that to experience
something as beautiful

                does not mean to experience it
necessarily wrongly—but that, too, is erroneous.

[Pause]

I want to believe that the effect of the beautiful,
according to Schopenhauer, has a calming effect
on the will.

[Pause]

        But this can occur only at close range,
           in close intimate contact.

        "A bracelet of bright hair about the bone"[12]

---

12. "Whispers of Immortality," in *Collected Poems and Plays,* T. S. Eliot, pp. 32, 33. Quoted from John Donne, "The Relique."

The shoulder lightly glazed with sand.

The salt-water smell of the flesh.

It's summer. No, it's Spring.
Your skin a pale white.

[Pause]

I want to believe that I've not sinned,
as St. Augustine suggests,
because I've lived too often
and too intensely
among the images of my mind

and yet I don't ask forgiveness

since those images also include
all the Redwing
Blackbirds and squirrels
and other powerful, sensual animals

that have gone thru enormous
transformations to reach me
because of the solitude
I do not share.

[Pause]

Rather, "love of beauty,"Nietzsche declares,
"can therefore be something other
than the *ability*
to *see* the beautiful,
create the beautiful. It can be
   an expression of the
      inability to do so."

envoi :

Any moment now I expect the crow
to come crashing through this dark windowpane
dizzy with sunlight and the earth wheeling
   and restless

It is the third of May.

It is early dawn.

It is the act of looking back.

It is the act of not looking back.

I did not invent you.

If only I knew where to find you,
I would surely find you.
But I don't know.

IV

SIGHTINGS

… looking at someone carries the implicit expectation that our look will be returned by the object of our gaze. Where this expectation is met […] the person we look at, or feels he's being looked at, looks at us in turn.

—Walter Benjamin,
from "On Some Motifs in
Baudelaire" (1939)

VISUAL DIALECTIC   [or "photographer unknown"

It is in the
        rapid
acquisition
    in the eyes—

                        everything else follows
                                from that,

                        and in a given instance,

something
beautiful
            about
a woman being
attentive to the
man she's with—

the reaching over
with napkin
        to wipe
the man's lips

the knees and/

or hands
touching

       under table   arm around shoulder

the alert, seemingly serious conversation
as though they are almost hidden—

the meaningful account of themselves

the *coup de foudre* on their faces.

       The time is 4:17

There is this isolated photo—

probably taken impromptu
   by street photographer—

as they were coming out of
the restaurant

but exactly *when*
cannot be determined

the negative is lost.
The print is of poor quality, pockmarked with grain.

The expressions of the faces barely readable,
so you can't make out the emotion
or perhaps what's said
    as they wait
        to cross the street—

                    the cool breeze
                        hitting the sides of the heads
                        before rain comes

will they separate
or go back to his rooms

will she stay the night
  or make excuse for
     leaving
        before daybreak, etc.

were they happy or lonely ?

will she deny fate,

thus negating what wld come after,

or how it wld not be
                    ten years after—having had her way

Could it have been Paris 1919 ?   (It feels like Paris

and being each other's only eyewitness
memory is inadequate, in this instance

or the compulsion to
turn experience itself
   into a way of seeing

is what
      survives
   as archival
      evidence.

               The few extant
                  photos of her
                     attributed to him, i.e.,

the one 8½ x 11 semi-gloss
printed full-neg,
               set on self-timer,

shoulder touching shoulder, full-face,

they look out
at those
who unknowingly chose
to be looked at
by looking
at them

               It is happening
                  all over again.

               for Eliane Kunzi
               and for Amedeo Modigliani

               4:vi:81 nyc

POEM IN THE MANNER OF PAUL BLACKBURN/MALANGA

Hitching up trousers

from having just gone to the can,

leaving the door purposely ajar—

beautiful, young girl

suddenly rushes in without knocking—whataya 'spect—

        shocked

at her surprise to find me there,

excuses herself   "That's all right" I say—

and suddenly leaves, a few seconds shared

in one lifetime of separate realities,

an erotic aftertaste.

        In another phantasy,

she wd've stayed,

got on her knees and sucked me off.

Her head held in my hands.

My hands running thru her hair

... shows what a cup of coffee can do in the morning.

31:v:90 Rte 22, Brewster, NY

... And maybe it wasn't 1932 :

In the photograph by
Laśzló Moholy-Nagy

is a young woman
leaning over deck
railing

with back to
camera

wch could be you

had it been you
in 1932
when this picture
was made.

SCENT

for
Sally
Mann, photographer

The poem
opens w/
Lee Miller
resting her head
on her father's
shoulder, Paris
January 1931
(Man Ray)

The poem
opens w/
children
lost in a
crowd of
voices after
school lets out

The mouth
is opening
and closing

Traces of saliva

give the brackets
their shine.

I prepare
for the poem
that will
never be
written

by picking up
the camera
instead

torn
denim

giving
way

at
the
knees

small, damp tendrils
of hair over neck
and ears

neck curving
gracefully
into collarbone

gentle curve

of spine

asleep
on bed

is a photograph

the cotton
tank-top
on back of
chair is a
photograph

What at first
appears clear
fades also,

past now
or ahead.

4:iv:89 nyc

THE BLACK BRA

for Kristen Westad

    My approach is not unlike that of Albert Pinkham Ryder
"soaking up the moonlight"

                         wch was his way   or the eye feeds
                                          on loveliness
                                              (Schaulust)

focusing in on
the black bra
beneath a sweatsoaked

               t-shirt
               of 100%
               durable
               cotton
                        against flesh

in,
of all places, Housatonic,

               a sleepy hollow
            as any you would imagine
                              to find
          in the fiction of
                   Nathaniel Hawthorne.

But let's get back to the black
bra

Let's get back to you
     to
        "seizing the moment"

        choice as recognition

        rolled-up shortsleeves,

        tendrils   of hair

        the skin translucent

        the face aglow

        the head
        back-lit

        the face that launched a thousand ships

        early morning rain and mist

        the Kamasutra and its variants

        picnics in a wheatfield

        skinnydipping the Green River

        Let's get back to
        history as
        point of focus
        in time,

to the black bra on the back of

a chair

30:vi:90 Housatonic, MA

Lorna Hopper, "Miss April" Playmate of the Month.

Who was Lorna Hopper ?:

Born: Fort Worth,
        lived in TX until 13.

        Her dad, a scientific researcher,
        moved the family to Manchester,
        Great Britain
        for two years.

        In 1965 the family moved to L.A.

Graduated high school, June 1968.
No notable dates,
except this one: Playboy Bunny
in the New Orleans Club, 1969,
at this time nineteen.

Lorna added to her income
from modeling, the
pursuit of
designing clothes. Says she:
"Every girl wants to
have a man who knows
how to

make her
feel like a woman."

To Lorna that means clothing
should always
be sensual, so the caption reads.

"In ancient times, the purpose of
clothes wasn't to hide nudity
but to decorate the body. End-quote.

The real Lorna is a shadowy figure.
For instance, the Lorna
presented in *Playboy*
is a person
of overwhelming beauty and power,
and assuming
how others respond to
her charm, her blush
is like the eclipse
of the Sun.
   Innocent
   in that light.

   In focus.

Lorna Hopper is an archetypal invention,
not unlike that of Beatrice,
appealing to the deepest emotions—

a vision received by the eyes

and later by the sense of smell
as found in fresh linen.

Apart from that
all that we know about her
is what Malanga himself tells us,
which may be largely imaginary,
or wch may be archival truth.

Now she recedes into the background
for nearly
        two decades,
until she reappears

       showing
herself
to the imagination
this poem defines,
        faithful to her
        being remembered :

Playboy, Vol. 16, no. 4—April 1969.

Slightly worn at the edges
w/ some creases.
        Otherwise
        entirely
        intact.

Someone's copy,
association unknown,
found at the Olive Tree

on the Rue Royale,
                    New Orleans.

It is, of course, years later.

3:iii:90 New Orleans, LA

CALVINIZED

for Josie Borain

    If I were writing a sonnet,
What would I put into the next eleven lines
Allowing the reader—myself—to know you(?),

though this could turn into something else:
the photo you made of you
nude in bathroom mirror,

a hotel perhaps,
                somewhere in Paris,

   morning prepping up
for a shoot,
or not that at all.

Little else would be known.
The rest is made up,
except what friends
would recall, if it came to that,

is how others see you. It matters
not that what was
to be a sonnet
turned somewhere else.

Here nothing's complete.

At exactly 10:30 a.m., a Wednesday,
April Fool's Day,
we look
without looking
anonymous to each other,

50th of a second, maybe two,
at the most.
A quick cut, a slow-motion freeze,
subway door shuts. Union Square.

You were wearing your basic black as I recall.

1:iv:92 nyc

What do they have in common?
That within distinct borders someone I loved
And someone I could easily love is sleeping.
That this poem can only invent what already exists
But lacking anything further
Becomes imagined again, becomes myth
And the idea of forgetfulness reverses itself.
To start with: the sweatshirt is turned
Inside out, the outside touching the skin.
A translucent, inner glow.
The hair blond and cropped short, so the
Back of the neck is fully exposed.
Seen at a distance, the Old Egremont Club, west
on Rte 23: lives in Boerum Hill, tests
Patients   HIV for a living—
Easily cld've been a fashion model. But no name.
Never got it. Never spoke a word to each other.
It's like Dante without Beatrice to be specific—
Not the unrequited sequence of events
Or the half-light of thirteenth century Italy,
But never knew she was being written about,
Watched from a small distance
On the Ponte Vecchio and then disappeared,
Like the girl with no name, like

The way someone you see once at a distance
Never leaves the mind's eye.
How long do you think before someone discovers you're who
I'm writing about?
We reshuffle the tearsheets endlessly,
Hoping the face might somehow change.
Now the past arrives and departs on the afternoon train
Out of Rome's Ottavia station. Then it was 1968.
I remember the way she looked,
Momently, halting in step,
As if in a slow-motion frieze frame
The middle of Piazza del Popolo,
The wide expanse of cobblestone reflecting bits of the sky.
She was hurrying to go somewhere.
There was so little to say and so nothing was said.
Amazing I've not given thought to Benedetta
Barzini all these years. Now suddenly
She's a person once again, like someone in 1991.
Suddenly Feltrinelli, her step-brother,
Calls out to me and I set back the clock
And he waits for me to come back.
The past is diminished.
Milano enveloped in the grey mist of an Ugo Mulas snapshot.
Milano a stone-gray of scaffolding, overhead wires,
Crowds of black umbrellas going every which way
In a futurist sunrise. Everything passes and fast.
Soon I'll forget what part Boerum Hill plays in all this.
Myth brings us back to where it all started,
Though irretrievable.
Memories someone else might read about,
Memories refusing to acknowledge personification.

History is like that.
Beatrice had no name.
You with *no-name*.
That's what we'll call you.
That's what I'm gonna have to call you.
Everything else is waiting to be invented …
Stories of passion,
Picture postcard vacations,
Prêt-à-porter soaked through from an afternoon shower
In the via Canova, a day
Unlike another, but soon, soon forgotten.
The mind drifting off into the mind's eye
Surrounded by what could be,
All my time occupied,
Without the faintest idea how to find you,
Because you exist as a face only.
No matter.
Reality is unreasonable sometimes.
No one needs to remember our unnamed lives—
A series of afterimages and
The evergreens undulate as the breeze
Is happening all the while, feeds into the landscape.
This morning's gold mist is compared with nothingness.
Last year the landscape was compared with nothingness.
Last year was still one year less …
But not now. Not now as the white tanktop strap
Slips from the white shoulder, disappears
In the b&w photo, becoming an afterthought,
Slightly underexposed.
Our time come and gone I suppose—
All that we know for sure happened as not happening.

The past gives away nothing. You have to research it.
Scent of travel, flesh of experience.
Something infinite is made finite again,
A matter of setting the f-stop, adjusting the focus,
The face vertically framed for the eternal last shot.
The longer you look at the face, it reveals nothing.
It's a matter how much of what we are
As history do we mean to believe
And how much is fantasy
The way what used to be isn't.
Empty flashbacks. Rooms filled with silence.
Last glint of sunlight in the hallway upstairs.
Somewhere in all this I know is my life:
The quiet, the sad Housatonic
Not more than 200 yards from where I now sit.
To my left Water Street Cemetery
With its tumbling granite obelisks, unfamiliar names
Like Keefe, Bracken, Giddings and Cosgrove,
Shadowed by tree limbs, a network of wires.
The past keeps erasing itself
And we all become no-names in a sense.
The neighbor's mower thrums till its almost music
Is that of a silence—roof silhouettes, a dog barking,
Traffic from Rte 7 beginning to thin.
Streetlights come on early
In Barrington against an indefinite twilight.
My favorite backroad is half-hidden, cluttered
With last year's leaves, this year's broken glass.
It's April again, and 1991 again,
Boerum Hill and Milano
And the Berkshires also come to think of it.

I can still imagine what it's like reliving the future
And now the sun comes out and I'm back in my chair.
See now ... I've almost forgotten her name,
The girl with no-name.

for Jed Weinberg

27:iv:91
Great Barrington, MA

Poem–before–epigraph (Poem)

Remnants of nothing

but this poem
        to account
     for,

     to be there alone,

     to remember,
     forget.

     Whatever time left
       quickly gone,

     emptied
     as it were,

     and no way back
     to beginning

     can ever retrieve
     what after all
     was only beginning

     suddenly

stopped: grey blue eyes,

shifting blue sky.
bright sun. Imagined
                photograph.

          And

                    ... one's pleasure
                    is always
                    partly accounted for
                    by the lack
                    of resemblance
                    between the desired object
                    and the discovery.
                    Whether
                    this discovery

[André Breton,   *be artistic,*
    from *L'Amour fou.*   *scientific,*
                    philosophic
                    or of
                    as mediocre
                    a use
                    as you please,
                    it takes
                    all the beauty
                    that I see in it
                    for what
                    it is not.

10:i:87 nyc

He went out quietly.

He is not with us anymore is what they will say
because no *one* person knows him in the same way.
He lent himself to a legend. Thus, suddenly
he ceased to have an identity to himself.
He put himself in this precarious and dangerous
situation of being adored or despised by people
who had never met him. Even his name evoked
reaction. One night I passed this person on
Lafayette Street, New York. He was going home
or what seemed to be going home. He was with
a beautiful young girl. Arms around shoulders,
they fitting into each other; but he seemed very much
alone ... isolated, in fact.

26:x:75 nyc

BEN MADDOW SPEAKS

for Tina Modotti

Her life turns up in many accounts
of Mexican life in the twenties.
She is a woman of great physical beauty
and personal dynamism.
Her best-known picture is the "Staircase"
taken in Mexico in the twenties.
She was a dedicated Communist—
in Mexico and in Moscow
and in Spain during the Civil War.

Born in northern Italy in 1896,
emigrated to San Francisco at age 17.
Four years later she married Ronbaix
(Robo) de l'Brie Richey.
They moved to Los Angeles.
She worked briefly as a starlet
in a number
of Hollywood movies.
She met Edward Weston.
She became his lover.
He encouraged her to take up photography.
He instructed her and was responsible
for the standards she observed.
She died in 1942 allegedly of a heart attack

in a taxi late one night,
in Mexico City,
although foul play was suspected
but could never be proved.

18:ii:89 nyc

L'Amour fou

A photocopy of the

Portrait of Natacha,

who was Man Ray's assistant at the time

when published in black and violet   *Harper's Bazaar*

(October 1940),

is tacked to the windowframe

East Mountain

where I look out now

•

but I as artiste have no such artifact

w/ wch to refer,

'cept what's in memory

your name,   for instance

Sarah Anderson,

or is it Natacha ?

———————————

The alternate ending

would be: We do meet,

negating all that wld come after—

at the very

least,

this

poem.

20:xii:92
Great Barrington, MA

SOME MEDIEVAL TROUBADOUR SONG, 14.xi.92, Cafe Flore, Paris.

I have caught a glimpse of Inès ...

Inès de la Fressange

at Cafe Flore

just as I'm leaving (let's dispense

w/ the *de la*)—

she stares back too, not knowing why. Quizzical.

No words are spoken, nor do I

stop to admire the beauty. (Eyes

fill with eyes)

Just as well,

otherwise the spell

wdve been broken. Instead,

Inès becomes a mythology

of the heart for a few

brief seconds. The net

is tight. Her hair wet

with early morning rain, jet

black, let

loose at shoulders—
just the right length,
that no wind momently touches.
After all, we're indoors.

Shape of
the little white t-shirt peeking thru
at cashmere neckline
                        revealed, my mind's

eye sees thru.
It is not summer.
I can only imagine
love's breasts, full-bodied, parfumed.

P A R F U M  I N è S

The firm ribcage and on down
thru the forests of night.
The quality of the flesh too,
                    so-called inner glow.
It's her eyes that get me though.

Fuck French politesse.
Hello, Inès!

Our histories sep'rate but true.

Then I go on
with my day
in this Parisian grey, soft rain,
toward blvd St-Michel,
run my fingers
thru the latest Cleo
Manara comix,
                    dreaming of pleasure,

thinking to ask, How is it you

are beautiful,
intelligent, perfect
to the eye ...
my own—not someone else's—I take pride,
something else I much needed to ask ...

but not now.

      Soon
I return—not to
Saint Germain des Prés
but to Massachusetts 01230 U S A
with Inès' onyx eyes in my head ...

eyes that will admit ...

nothing.

      Close but far.

      Respectful, in fact.

      That's how we are.

      "separate réalités"

But for this one moment

we may never

cross eyes again,

smile.

In this way time emerges,

suspended in time.

Inès, what time is it now, three?

December almost

3 in the afternoon, almost.

Nothing looks more like inspiration
than the way you come into the room.
It's true and I don't give a damn.
It's said from the painting by Balthus a figure at times emerges,
like a young girl nude from a mirror.
But how would I know this?
Is it your fate to be tricked by the flesh?
Is it any better to be thrown into this poem,
which begins in the predawn light
before waking? Suddenly it's snowing in Stuttgart.
Suddenly I've arrived at this point of departure
in a friend's car with the sound of the windshield wipers.
A falcon soars above East Mountain.
That much I can make out.
A sudden downpour
turns everything pink and grey on Railroad Street.
The sound of the typewriter keys
is the impression of all that's unsaid.
After twenty years you're asked the meaning of beauty.
After twenty years you become someone else.
There are no eye-witnesses;
only what the eye sees and the photographs.

14:iv:95 Great Barrington, MA

THE INVISIBLE PHOTOGRAPHS

What many cannot forget are her eyes.
She stands, feet planted firmly, the body
profiled on the far left of a grainy black & white photo.
Or she's standing wide-eyed behind a steamy pane of blue glass.
One hand touching the window through clouds.
The nape of a neck that rises steeply,
the tender curve of the skin behind the ear.
The hair close-cropped.
These are your attributes. These are your mysteries.
That's how Dick Avedon described you.
He said the mirror looks at you,
so the mirror looks at you.
You collect yourself.
Carefully, as if buttoning a shirt—the last button,
you compose your features.
It's a whole communion of perfumes and phrases,
of thoughts and of breathing. The eyes now averted.
The exposure double-checked: 60th at f/5.6 or eleven.
The film-speed is grainy and fast.
Rumpled tanktop.
The mauve light washing the walls.
I have never, to my mind, known anyone named Alexis Barth.

19:iii:95
Great Barrington, MA

V

FASHION SECRETS

This was an overwhelming desire for possession, this was an inerasible printing of the girl's face on his brain and he knew she would haunt his memory every day of his life if he did not possess her. His life had become simplified, focused on one point, everything else was unworthy of even a moment's attention.

—Mario Puzo
from *The Godfather*

STUDIO
54

for   Anton

Quarter
past four,

midnight

time coming
from the past

Now it changes.

Faces
specifically
human

Flora McEwen—

"lovely to look at"

song to be remembered

dancing the night away

recalling some thing
or someone after

Chill in air

pre-dawn light

city asleep
or else, possibly
waking

night coming to
an end, always.

8:vi:78 nyc

Rimbaud: *L'amour est a reinventer.*

Gia Carangi

One no longer picks up a copy

of American VOGUE

with your picture,

with your hair pushed back

away from forehead and

face is how you're best

photographed,

or it's a series of contactsize prints

of posture changing reflections

or it all begins to end in a photo somewhere.

Xmas 1989

Punk appropriation of Irving Penn's photograph
Benedetta Barzini, ca. 1966.
Photo © by Gerard Malanga, 1982.

A NEWLY DISCOVERED FASHION POEM: 1967

for Benedetta in 1992

Here's balance: this
walking skirt and this easy-
fitting length of jacket
that stops just where the pleats break,
gives them room
to start swinging.

And here's balance: it runs
like an invisible cord,
right up the centre of this lithe
body, straight all the way—ankles
through pelvis through head.
Held as it should be, directly
over the shoulders. Try it: use
your earrings as a guide; imagine
they're dangling
on the tendon just back of the neck.
You'll find you're moving your head
back a little,
shoulders a bit forward—and
balancing with ease.

discovered 5:viii:92

POEM IN ITALIAN

DONNA GIADA RUSPOLI,

youngest beauty of a princely Roman family ... tall,

slender, seventeen; daughter of Don Sforza and Donna

Domitilla Ruspoli. She has flowing dark-gold hair, violet-

blue eyes, side-set in a fantastic sweep of lashes. In her

face now are the reserve and mystery of youth; in her body,

its quick grace and energy ... For this photograph

by Avedon, Donna Giada wore makeup

for the fourth time in her life.

12:vi:90
Great Barrington, MA

What Becomes a Duchamp Most

for Zoé

Are you a sweetheart

Are you a tom-boy

Are you tangible

Are you a tangle of hair

Are you waking up now

Are you lovely to look at

Is your face turned sideways

Are you a champagne of shoulders

Are you straight from the shoulder in a fresh cool shirt

youthful head
catching rays of the sun
lycéenne, main stairwell, Genève

breast slightly arched you lean over the rail

Are you photogenic like that

Are you concealed

Are you the girl on a swing
moving through sky with clouds for a backdrop
with hair let loose like flags of ecstasy

Are you a femme-enfant

Are you an apache

Are you a rushing river a murmuring sound

smiles of a summer night

odor of musk

the long eyes with their tremulous glances

Are you the eyes of a young deer

Are you the pure light of the navel

pure light of the soul

Are you the dream of Duchamp

the dream of Rrose Sélavy

Are you the leg smooth the foot naked

the nude descending a staircase

nude semi-disrobed

Are there towels   Are you sunlight

Are you sunlight streaming through a warren of pine
and a crisp cool breeze

and the song of crickets

Are you melting

Are you the melting
of the wave
on the
breast of
a calm sea
shoulder deep, backlit in the photo

Are you the hazy autumn sun

Are you the "beauté convulsive"
André Breton once spoke of
not thinking to ask

Are you a state of mind anyway

Are you none of the above

Are you Paris emerging from dawn

Are you Paris dreaming

Do you imagine

Are you a Patek Philippe

Are you L'Amour courtois

Are you L'Amour fou

Are you electric

Above all are you electric

You push the black hair back from your forehead,
which is bony.
I can still see your hand as you do it.

24:iv:94
Great Barrington, MA

Uma Thurman's breasts

A new poem doesn't begin all of a sudden,

nor are Uma Thurman's breasts

what this poem's about—

not the three diamonds. Right? Right.

     Story has it a young man
removes his glass eye
from the socket
as far as the eye can see
flings it
        into the overturned lake
and to never repeat it—somewhere
from the ends of the earth, somewhere

the Himalayas

a raincloud hides everything for a moment

above the cloud there is nothing

the lake loses reflection

people unacquainted gather,

but by then the student had vanished

and from the ricochet
was born an incomparable
                                silence

The rest is not known

───► 4-sec. FADE

Now some years later
You are not yet ten, You
are not yet You

You open the window wide
Trees leafy thick and light diffused
splinters of sunlight, the play of light
on the sidewalk out front.

Here's your young street, all perspired now

College Street, Amherst

and you're only a little girl still
Your mom dresses you in blue and white,
like summer white blue and white

but not now

You are pasting pictures into small copybooks.

You are skipping rope and counting

braids bouncing

floral dress, cap sleeves

flared above knees

skirt catching the light, breeze

caressing the skirt

You are filling in with your box of colors

You are enclosed in dream

You remembered back then

You got up you
got out of the train

Your cat watches in darkness
perched on the sill

We're back on the street,

quiet, suburban.

Thunderous roar of the Montreal freight
at six in the morning rattles the windows asleep

Sleeping

Waking

Blue eyes bright teeth red lips

looking straight into the camera for a kiss

Wake-up call.

A room filled with sunlight.

You're supposed to roam alone in the fragrance
of evening, just like you dreamed it.
You're supposed to make-believe

even now.
You are fourteen years old.

Hide and Go Seek
Count to 10
Ready or Not,
Here I Come!

Uma and her friend
idle against a billboard
at the end of an empty street
under stormy skies

and the wind shudders along the sidewalk

and puddles of water, ruts

in the road,

dead cigarette butts

but not now

There it is the young street and you
still but a small child
Lemon-fresh

The rain washed down on you

And wet eyes learn to smile again.

This AnscoColor print

contains all the future

looking back at a past.

She's to the right in the picture.

She covers her face with an infinite mask,

    then removes it.

She is dark, cool and serene

She appears happy or sad

She is secretive

It's a picture hung in a museum
And every once in a while on school trips to the city
you get up close and examine it

Which one ?

The ten likely pictures she
would have
posed for: Cranach. Cranach's The Three Graces,
the one on the right,
with aquiline nose,

tender little-half-smile, head looking back, awe-struck

Manet's Gare Saint-Lazare

The Age of Innocence, the bois

de Boulogne, Pierre Auguste Renoir

Robert Doisneau,

the exception: Paris in half-darkness

               Paris buzzing with sunlight

resurrection of flesh

and bodies of knowledge

some such thing

"The Lady with the Unicorn"

not a painting, a series of tapestries.

The section called *Sight*.

You are wearing a summer dress and you take it off.

You wrap yourself in a cloud.

Your hands merge

into the white of your breast.

The three gentle folds at your belly

intensify, subside.

The camera pulls back.

Somehow
it all comes back to the young man
with the one real eye ...

There are limits to what one can imagine,
so we do everything with our eyes
The eye that seizes the mouth and kisses it

Eyes that turn into dawn
Eyes of passing women throughout life

It will be the same as in this life,
The same lane in the forest where the sun barely breathes,
And at midday, in mid–autumn
When the clean road turns like a young girl
To gather the valley flowers,
We will cross in our walks,
    As in the yesterday you have forgotten,
    In the skirt whose color you have forgotten.

CUT!

Ok, break for lunch, be back and ready at 2.

16:v:94
Great Barrington, MA

VI

WHO ARE WE
NEXT TIME?

Freud, knowing what he felt the need
of—love—knew what others needed. He
realized, too, that we must not repress
aggressiveness. Life must be made into
loving aggressiveness; aggression sweetened
by love. Thus one can be killed in an easier
fashion, die a very easy death: a ritual death.

—Eugene Ionesco,
from *Fragments of a Journal*

Vase with flowers

Fate has it the world didn't exist
as when you meet someone—the
occurrence of that period
                    in some such way
as this
termed "meaningful coincidence,"
recognized as such
                    the choice
to deny or fulfill   the fear also

Leaves all gone now. Sky's crisp and clear.
Skin bronzed in the shaded light.

This is the world of the imagination.
This is a photo of Virginia
last year in Amsterdam.

1:i:94 Great Barrington, MA

WRITING FROM MEMORY

I'm trying to write this photo
from memory

the selfportrait
through mirror
reversing eyes,

so the face is your own
but not its reflection

so looking at you
is looking at me
or vice versa

> Imagine
> seeing the verso
>
> of this picture
>
> is the back of the head,
>
> tendrils of hair, the neck
>
> parfumed

and on down
the small of the back,

the pubic arch
smoothly curving under—

but I'm not standing

back

of you

My vision makes you life-like

as in the photo life-like

you've made

of yourself.

*for Virginia Vincent,
in Paris.*

22: iii:93
Great Barrington, MA

The visionary is the only true realist.

—*Federico Fellini,*
1992 Academy Awards Ceremony.

Mythologies of the heart and to Virginia Vincent,
   photographer

   The look, it's been told, is the
most immediate manifestation of desire.

Duchamp's desire to go beyond Cubism

can already be seen

in a canvas of this period;

portrait★ of a woman
passing by: a girl glimpsed once, loved
and never seen again.

Orson Welles says much the same—"Citizen Kane":

not a day has gone by that he hasn't thought of
that girl,
         or William

★ "Portrait" (Dulcinea), 1911 (Av. de Neuilly—16th Arrondissement,
Neuilly sur Seine).

Carlos Williams—he saw

what we see: girl at street corner
                 waiting for light to change
                 in the dead-heat of summer,
                 the side of her breast
                 glimpsed through cut-out and back-lit—

"Her
      hips were narrow, her
                              legs
thin and straight. She stopped

me in my tracks—until I saw
her
      disappear in the crowd" ofttimes quoted.

                         Likewise experienced.

A throw of the dice ... a vision in time.

              Alighieri, too, was obsessed
           with the sight of Beatrice.
A day in thirteenth-century Florence,

on the Ponte Vecchio,

seeing her at close range. For you

there's no like-adventure. You are not

stranger; you are not

someone seen
and not spoken to You are not
eyes meeting eyes.

And entirely different set of circumstances arise,

fated as such—"What's your name?" ... and quickly

you vanish into Parisian night rain,

not knowing and knowing
                    What appears real
                    is different from what either of us
                    imagined. So the outcome
                    I desire and what you feel within
                    form a reality proportionate
                    to our creative involvement.

A fusion of opposites, of separate realities.

Morning after: the circularity

of our look that looks at us naked, tangled in bedsheets

and sunlight. An endless instant. The Nikon,

pre-focused, set on self-timer. Whose camera?

8:iv:93 Great Barrington, MA

ENDANGERED SPECIES

This is not a picture of Kay Boyle and
          Harry Crosby
      at Le Moulin du Soleil
   Ermenonville, France, Winter, 1929.
That one can be found in the
Special Collections / Morris Library
Southern Illinois University, Carbondale.
This one was made in the photomaton,
6^e Arrondissement, near Cafe Flore.
Perhaps it's the way they don't look at each other
makes everyone believe that there's
real incompatibility between them.
Misappropriated, mislabelled
until eighty years later,
it's the only proof that they were together.

26:xii:93 Red Rock, NY

SOME THINGS TO REMEMBER ABOUT TRI-X

... but not everything is that predictable:

The wet heat of an armpit, for instance

handsome breasts rising

fingers that touch

slope of back, shoulders

caressing the feet, the hands

the smell of all that goes
    into memory of self

hand resting on thigh

ankles crossed   ,   naked eyes

Sound of wind through tops of trees
    in Reineke's yard

and there were birds this morning
early and a bit of rain too

the secret parfum

the questions are not wrong

And there are magical differences too.
She smokes. I don't. Cigarettes, that is

And someone holds her face up
          for a kiss

and days later someone
can't quite get to sleep—*wonder who that is?*

Finally the stars
flicker and go out.

A dream is waking

        So
it's not very strange
that the photo is always there
when one looks out the window, it
being morning

and to see clouds and mountains
in the motionless distance ...

                    I am back at my "spot"

not the Weesperzijde. 2 Anderson Street.

Time is racing.

What time is it now?

The cats move quietly about the house.

A wind comes in from the north
      but softly.

The mountains fade into light.

Old hawk-eye circles above

I rise early

coffee, my first cup of the day,

stare out at East Mountain

Try not to think. Laugh inside.

What do all these things
      have to do with photography?

What do all these things have
      in common?

On the Weesperzijde, A'dam
28:v:93

for Virginia Vincent

18 February 1994

---

not the 19th is André Breton's birthday

acknowledged founder of Surrealism

which would have made him 98 today

but that's not the real reason

for writing this poem

There's this snapshot see a moment when it's completely dark
When a cloudbank passes in front of the sun
So André his wife Elisa their heads back-lit
In open shade the white oak singing the heated begonias
It appears they have just finished lunch
On a hillock sloping out back
A friend's cottage in Neuilly sur Seine
They have their differences but they have a life
Together that is to say they're wearing each other's pyjamas
Here he continually turns back on his childhood
As primary source for the dream
And she

When she bends down

I can see her breasts caressed by shadows of light
Through the folds of the blouse
Her beauty spills over
Warm and parfumed areolae bronze-like in color
The day is beautiful
Broad-shouldered tendrils of hair
Free-flowing over her face
Blaise Cendrars once remarked
Elisa has the most beautiful breasts in the world
"Le corse lot," is how he put it

Others characterize her as leger trompeur
Factice sans sincere

She has no fear
Of loving or of taking
She also knows how to give
Often I imagine what it might've been like
He had written a poem, "My Wife"
It's supposed to've appeared
An edition of three dedicated to Marcel
Duchamp whose favorite number *is* 3
But none survive and the manuscript has never been found

I study the photograph for a long time
Elisa appears to be dark and quiet and serious
Her eyes even look down perhaps avoiding glare
Of the two o'clock sun this picture bears
A striking resemblance to others
In the history of photogenic romance

So there's this deep solitude in her face

I noted passing her once in the R. des Archives (3^e)
Elisa speaks to no one I'm told
She won't even come to the phone what gives
She came from a broken home brother mother no one else
She remembers nothing else
Was she a nice person is pure speculation
She's less a character than continual temptation
But the game is up she never played fair

She roamed the quais at night
And photographed street gangs preying on tourists
She'd bum a cigarette now and then even after
She quit smoking her teeth had gone yellow

It's alleged Elisa once asked of her husband,

     "Who will replace us?"

André's answer: "Who knows, maybe no one."

Can it be, the 22nd already ...

———————————————————

One year after.

That fateful night.

Sparndammerstraat, the morning after.

Fresh bite on neck. Wet-eyed.

Looking for breakfast, waiting for Gaëlle.

Your gutsiness was admirable,
your curiosity sublime,
more remarkable
                    for your strength of mind,
than for whatever chastity
you hope to achieve by default.

"Amused,"

as Duchamp would say.

For an instant you won't know who you are,

coming all that way from Paris by bus,

brief encounter, just like in life,

and to be smug in that fact.
                              What did you expect:

                              Alain Bashung.

     You got André Malraux

with Beretta 92 cocked.

Or: Ira suggests,
                    playing Virgil to my Dante,

"She shd've arrived without underwear on,

as proof of sincerity." Show me! Show me!

So she missed the joke as sincere,

                    so she sashays anyway.

Is it the 22nd already? The promise of nothing.

Have to go back to Nikon Address Book 1993,
                    the one I scribble in,
check the date,

Friday—no, a Saturday.

                    Have to

flesh out T. S. Eliot's theory
of metaphysical poetry
                              to illustrate
"the dissociation of object,
feeling and thought ..." etc. Imagine.

                    What's this got to do with *a life* ?
Nothing.

So she made a mundane mistake.

        Have to do a total sweep of the house,
empty the trash,
be sure the lawn-mower's running—
but I don't.

        Instead, redefine
and subdivide a simple emotion,
such as *within the memory*,

so the grass grows,

so the letters turn into notes and then nothing,

so it's not five years. Let's pretend.

So ... so what. So who gives a shit.

                    Instead,
clearly location the emotion,
examine the minute particulars
of my daily life,

my quotidian mind
(had to look that one up!)
primarily perhaps my way of love-making,
which is not to say how,
                    but also
any activity—
my optimist surge.
                    My inner rage,

                    innate curiosity.

"... a month hasn't gone by since ..." (*Citizen Kane*)

Can I reconcile the real with the mythic?

Reinvent the future?

Imagine snapshots into existence?

Suddenly I'm halfway through all this without a title:

                    Asi Que Pase Un Año,

inadvertently discover in my Cassell's
that *ano*, w/out tilde over the *n*
is decidedly *anus*—that's funny.

The root of it then.

            It can also mean ring, annular,

as in annular ligament—a fibrous
band that rings the ankle
or wrist joints.
                    A delicate balance

of the third of the three diamonds,

if the light is right,

the back of the wrist
                    where parfum performs,

or place a kiss on that wrist,

so it's not 7 types of ambiguity after all,

so it's called, "once one year past,"

so: once upon a time ... Amsterdam,

so this is
where it all started: a spring day once one year past,

passes into thought;
                    and this thought,
far from attaining *belief*,
is immediately
                    the object of another feeling!
What feeling?

A city dreaming of Paris. A pre-dawn.

A wet street. Café noir.

A bare, round shoulder.

Shop window reflecting a face, two faces, whatever else.

Suddenly you're somebody else.

Suddenly I'm wakened.

My two cats find their spot on the bed again and dream.

It's six in the morning.

Outside, the muffled silence of snow falling.

A bicycle lightly covered in snow.

A house dwarfed by a mountain.

A road which leads to a dead-end.

It's spring now.

Amsterdam: Is it a short history

of a small place?

Is it the curse

of the romantic to go on dreaming?

Is it rolling fields of clover and a white, morning mist?

Is it other worlds than this?

Is it something permanent,

like non-events that go on drifting

in time, because we believe them to happen?

Is it what not happens?

Is it "mapping the war zones

of the heart," as Freud liked to point out?

What was he thinking, I wonder?

Was it raining that day in Worcester, Mass.,

    or was that Hampstead, North London?

    Not every day

personal history repeats itself—dashed

on the rocks.

Not every day, one or the other denies

what could come after.

Not every day

a mundane mistake sets history on its side,

so that Picasso's Woman in White need not have existed.

Not every day.   If you,

                    if you,

like you the reader,
                    may call the thought "insincere,"

because it does not reach belief, doesn't happen ...

And this isolation of

thought as an object

of sense ... of thought as object of desire

could hardly

be possible

before May 22nd,

a Saturday,

1993 ...

22:vi:94
Great Barrington, MA

for Gaëlle and for Ira

RETURN TO PARIS AFTER TWO YEARS

Paul Blackburn, his line :

To create the situation / is love

and to avoid it, this is also

Love.

Fate being a double-edged sword

What if ... what if

the situation be repeated again:

You're running, see ?

before the doors close at Galerie Donguy

You're running half out of breath

the Rue de la Roquette,
in the fading light, the chill air.
You are dodging the evening shoppers,

swinging out toward the curb edge,

standing in the street simply.

An apple, orange, deux cahiers.

You have your Nikon wrapped in plastic

to keep from getting wet,

but then you arrive.

The lights are out   (next time maybe.

Everyone has since left,

so the photos we have of

each other are not of

each other,

as if the past were anything else but

what it is. Luck is

always for tomorrow. Luck is

starcrossed. Luck is

something forever gone and again renewed.

So-called "chapter" you once said,

to begin anew,

to grow from that—and

repeated often enough

even the word looks empty, despite the hope,

despite the smell of hot flesh.

It is not Spring in Amsterdam.

It is the Month of the Photo in Paris.

It is again 1992.

It is windless here.

No, it does not rain.

I called out to her,

feel the warmth

and as she turned,

I suddenly woke.

15:xii:94 Paris.

Printed January 1996 in Santa Barbara
& Ann Arbor for the Black Sparrow Press by
Mackintosh Typography & Edwards Brothers Inc.
Text set in Bembo by Words Worth.
Design by Barbara Martin.
This edition is published in paper wrappers;
there are 200 hardcover trade copies;
100 hardcover copies have been numbered & signed
by the author; & there are 26 lettered copies
handbound in boards by Earle Gray each with an
original signed photograph by Gerard Malanga.

Photo © 1995 Asako

GERARD MALANGA, poet, photographer and filmmaker, worked closely with Andy Warhol during the artist's most creative period in the mid-Sixties. His several books of poetry, ranging from *chic death* (1971) to *Three Diamonds* (1991), have earned him worldwide recognition.

In addition, Malanga's other works include UPTIGHT: *The Velvet Underground Story*, co-authored with Victor Bockris (1983), and the feature-length screenplay *Cinéma parlant* (1993), translated into French by Anne Guillemard. *Seizing the Moment*, a monograph of his photo-portraits, is presently being prepared for publication, with essays by Ben Maddow and Peter K. Wehrli.

Gerard Malanga has travelled widely, and divides his time between New York and the Berkshires, in western Massachusetts. He is currently an honorary Fellow at Simon's Rock of Bard College, and serves on the executive board of The Akashic Record, a non-profit foundation for the arts.